laws. This caused many problems between the states.

Congress followed the Articles of Confederation, signed by the thirteen colonies during the Revolutionary War, but the laws did not allow Congress to collect taxes, issue paper money, regulate trade, or make treaties. The Congress did not have the power it needed to build a strong nation.

A change was needed, but the people could not agree on what the change should be. The Federalists wanted more power for Congress. The Antifederalists, however, feared a strong central government. They had just fought a long war to be free of England's powerful rule.

James Madison ▶

James Madison and Alexander Hamilton, who were both Federalists, made plans for a meeting of the states. Hamilton wrote a letter to say that a meeting would be held in Philadelphia on May 14, 1787. This meeting was to "take into consideration the situation of the United States." It was to be called the Constitutional Convention.

James Madison, from Virginia, was 36 years old and always dressed in black. Although he was only five-feet, four-inches tall, he towered over the other men at the meeting in scholarship and wisdom. This is why he became known as "The Father of the Constitution."

THE GREAT AMERICANS SERIES

Men of the Constitution

By Pamela Bradbury

Illustrated by James Seward

A Wanderer Book
Published by Simon & Schuster, Inc. New York

Cover Portrait: Four By Five Inc.

▲ Philadelphia as it appeared just after the Revolutionary War.

By the 1780s the American Revolution had already been fought and won. The Liberty Bell was ringing in Philadelphia, and Betsy Ross had made the first flag of stars and stripes. There were thirteen proud new states.

But the new United States of America had a problem despite its independence from Great Britain—the states were *not* united. Instead, each one acted separately and made its own

Alexander Hamilton, thirty-two, was a small man who was brilliant, handsome and dashing. Born in the British Leeward Islands in the Caribbean, he had come to New York as a boy. He saw things more clearly than some Americans because he was not attached to any state, but to a nation of united states.

As a young soldier during the Revolution, he wrote a bold letter to the Congress. His message was clear—Congress must have full power to act. The war had not yet ended, and he was already making plans for his country. He had a vision of what the Constitution of the United States was to become.

National Portrait Gallery, Smithsonian Institution, Washington, D.C.

◄ Alexander Hamilton

The excitement about the meeting began to grow when the states learned that America's greatest hero, George Washington, was going to the Constitutional Convention.

Deciding to go to the convention was not easy for Washington. The six-foot, two-inch man had served his country well. During the Revolution, Washington found out how much America needed a strong central government. He and his troops spent a very cold winter at Valley Forge, with little food and few warm clothes. Washington learned that Congress had no money for shoes and no power to get it! How could a country become a strong nation if it did not have the power to get shoes for its soldiers?

After six years of fighting, Washington went home to Mount Vernon, Virginia. He no longer wanted to take part in government, but to enjoy his family, friends and home.

Now just four years later, he was fifty-five years old and at

the height of his national popularity. Because people trusted and loved him, they begged him to represent Virginia at the Philadelphia meeting. Although he longed to be at home, he knew his beloved country would not last if a stronger union was not formed.

◄ Benjamin Franklin

When George Washington arrived in Philadelphia on Sunday, May 13th, the first visit he made was to Pennsylvania's representative, Benjamin Franklin. Franklin brought his worldwide reputation to the convention. Franklin was a short, stout man whose white hair fell on the shoulders of his plain Quaker clothes.

Although Franklin's parents had been poor and he had little formal schooling, he was always an avid reader. He owned his own printing shop and newspaper, and had started the first lending library. He enjoyed writing and printing Poor Richard's Almanac, a special calendar that told what the weather would be like. Each page also had a wise saying such as "A true friend is the best Possession."

◄ George Washington arriving in Philadelphia

Franklin stopped working at age forty-two. He was happiest when he was experimenting, inventing and spending time with his family. He served many years as a member of the Pennsylvania Assembly and as a spokesman for all of America in Europe. The people in France loved him! He was a world famous writer, scientist, and statesman.

Now, at eighty-one, he was ready to go to the most important meeting in America's young history. He could no longer walk the short distance from his house to the State House, so he was carried in a box-like sedan chair. His body was weak, but his mind was still sharp.

The Convention could not begin on May 14th as planned. All the men were not yet there. Some were still sailing along the coast, others were coming by horseback. The New Hampshire delegates had not even started their trip because their state could not afford to send them.

As the delegates from Pennsylvania and Virginia waited for the others, they were kept busy. George Washington was the guest at many parties, operas and concerts. James Madison met with the other Virginia delegates and read more of the books that Thomas Jefferson had sent him. Although Jefferson was in France and could not come to the Convention, he had sent what Madison called a "literary cargo" of books.

The Convention finally opened on Friday, May 25, with nine states represented. Even though fifty-five men were involved, the usual daily count was thirty. These leaders were planters,

Independence Hall ▶

lawyers, doctors, businessmen, college professors and men of leisure. Most had had experience in government, and more importantly, they knew that the survival of the young nation depended on their work.

George Washington was quickly chosen as presiding officer. This respected man showed the importance of the work to come when he said, "If to please the people we offer what we ourselves disapprove, how can we afterwards defend our work? Let us raise a standard to which the wise and honest can repair. The event is in the hands of God."

To many of the representatives, work of this importance was not new. Elbridge Gerry, an Antifederalist from Massachusetts, had helped frame the Articles of Confederation. Both John Dickinson, a scholarly Federalist from Delaware, and Robert Morris, a good natured famous businessman, had also signed the Articles of Confederation.

Charles Cotesworth Pinckney was a young Federalist from South Carolina. As a member of the 1786 Congress, his request for a revision of the Articles of Confederation was turned down.

Scottish-born James Wilson was a scholar who argued beautifully for the Federalists. This signer of the Declaration of Independence also knew the importance of the work that lay ahead.

James Madison took careful notes every day during the four months of meetings. Every night he wrote out his notes with a quill and ink. He told a friend, "The labor

. . . almost killed me." His notes were first made public after his death and are among the most valuable historical records of the United States.

Many steps were taken to ensure the success of the meetings. The delegates agreed that everything said must be kept secret. This way, men could say what they thought without worrying about newspaper reports. There were guards posted outside the door. And the cobblestone streets were covered with straw so the passing horses and wagons would not disturb them.

▼ James Wilson

Edmund Randolph ▶

On May 29, the young, good looking Edmund Randolph proposed the Virginia Plan. Madison and the other Virginia men had been working on it while waiting for the convention to begin. The plan called for a strong central government with a two-house legislature representing the states according to their populations. The lower house would be elected by the people and the upper house would be elected by the lower house. A President would be chosen by the legislature. There would be a Supreme Court and lower courts. There were many debates about this plan.

The smaller states were alarmed that the more populated states would have so much power. Two weeks later, William Paterson proposed the New Jersey Plan. The five-foot, two-inch, Irish-born Antifederalist was said to have "the inward-looking eyes of a thinker." "Judge" Paterson, as he was called, favored keeping the states at the center of things. His plan kept the Articles of Confederation but gave Congress the power to tax and regulate commerce. It also proposed a multi-person Presidency, with a Supreme Court and lower courts.

Paterson feared for New Jersey. He said, "She will be swallowed up!" After the New Jersey Plan was defeated, Paterson remained at the convention to help work on a compromise.

Roger Sherman, a rural shop keeper from Connecticut, was an Antifederalist. He wanted each state to have one vote regardless of its population. Deciding how many votes a state should have caused so many problems that the convention almost failed because of it.

In mid-July Sherman, who was a signer of the Declaration of Independence, offered the Great Compromise. Representatives to the lower house would be elected according to the size of the state's population.

But in the Senate, each state would be equally represented by one Senator. This compromise was accepted by the delegates.

The delegate who did the most talking was pegged-legged Gouverneur Morris, a Federalist from Pennsylvania. He made 173 speeches! His listeners were sometimes shocked or angry, but never bored. The tall, brilliant man was also witty and quite wealthy.

One night at dinner, he boasted that he was not afraid of General Washington and to prove it, he would slap Washington on the back. People were shocked. The next day, he decided to just put his hand on Washington's arm. Later Morris said, "The great man turned and looked at me, and I wished the earth had yawned and swallowed me up!"

▲ Gouverneur Morris

These men and many others worked very hard to write the Constitution. They were away from their homes for four, hot, rainy months. They missed their families. They spent six days a week working in a closed room in hopes of making a better government. Because of their dedication, they are called the nation's Founding Fathers.

Their final debate began on August 10. They approved two-year terms for Representatives, six-year terms for Senators, and four- year terms for the President. The powers of the President, the Congress and the Courts were also written.

On September 17, the work was complete. Benjamin Franklin spoke urging "every member . . . who may still have objections to it, would with me . . . put his name to this instrument."

George Washington was the first to sign followed by men from each of the other states represented. In all, thirty-nine of the original fifty-five signed the new Constitution. Of the remaining

George Mason ▶

sixteen, most were simply not in Philadelphia on that day. Three who were pre-
sent, however, refused to sign. Governor
Randolph of Virginia feared that the President had too many powers and would rule
like a king. George Ma-
son, also of Virginia,
and Elbridge Gerry of
Massachusetts felt
strongly that the Con-
stitution should include
a declaration of rights.

Courtesy of the Library of Congress, Washington, D.C.

The Founding Fathers wrote a constitution for a very young country. No one knew whether the Constitution would survive all the problems that the growing country would have, but they made sure that new laws could be added as they were needed. They made sure that Congress had the power to protect America when it was in danger. They made sure that the government was by the people, and they made sure the union of states was preserved.

The men returned home to show the Constitution to the people they represented. Alexander Hamilton and James Madison wrote letters in the newspapers telling how the Constitution corrected the weaknesses of the Articles of Confederation.

Delaware was the first state to ratify the new Constitution. In Massachusetts and New

York, there were great debates. In Virginia the patriot Patrick Henry, who had refused to attend the Convention, spoke strongly against the Constitution. Finally in June, 1788, enough states had ratified it to make it the law of the land. Colorful parades were held all over the country to celebrate!

But while some people were celebrating, others were already at work on an addition to the Constitution that would protect the rights and liberties of the people. James Madison prepared the Bill of Rights which still protects the American people today.

After the Constitution became the law of the land, many of the Founding Fathers returned to what they had been doing. Others had jobs in the new government.

George Washington became the first President of the United States.

Alexander Hamilton was chosen to be the first Secretary of the Treasury.

Edmund Randolph became the first Attorney General.

James Madison was elected the fourth President of the United States. Under his leadership, Congress declared war against Britain in 1812. The War of 1812 proved that the United States could defend itself.

Benjamin Franklin continued inventing until his death at age eighty-four.

Gouverneur Morris was sent to London as a special envoy of President Washington's to determine

▲ Ben Franklin at work.

whether treaties between Britain and the United States were possible. He was a United States Senator from 1800–1803.

Roger Sherman was elected by the people to serve two years as a Representative. He also served two years as a Senator before his death.

"Judge" Paterson served in the first United States Senate and was an associate judge of the Supreme Court. His decisions as a judge helped to establish the constitution as law of the land.

Thousands of people visit the National Archives Building in Washington, D.C. each year. They stand in awe of the Founding Fathers who had the courage to write:

"We the People of the United States, in order to form a more perfect union, establish justice, insure domestic tranquility, provide for the common defense, promote the general welfare, and secure the blessings of liberty to ourselves and our posterity, do ordain and establish this Constitution of the United States of America."